The
Thingumajig
Book of
Health
and
Safety

Story by
Irene Keller

Illustrations by
Dick Keller

Ideals Publishing Corp.
Milwaukee, Wisconsin

Copyright © MCMLXXXII by Dick and Irene Keller
Milwaukee, Wisconsin 53201
All rights reserved. Printed and bound in U.S.A.
Published simultaneously in Canada.
ISBN 0-8249-8031-X

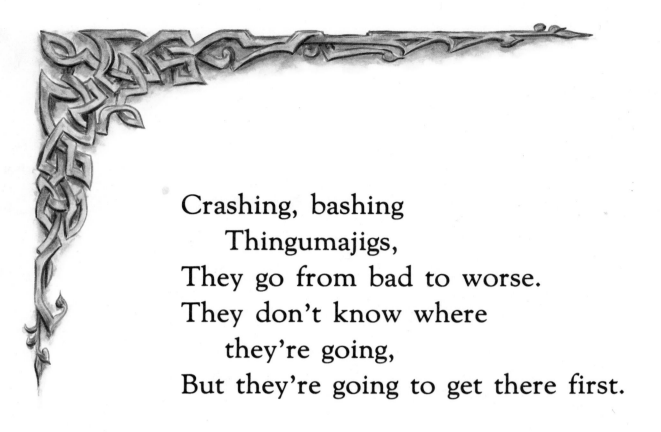

Crashing, bashing
  Thingumajigs,
They go from bad to worse.
They don't know where
  they're going,
But they're going to get there first.

I always give hand signals
And keep to the right as well.
I walk my bike at crossings
And always use my bell.

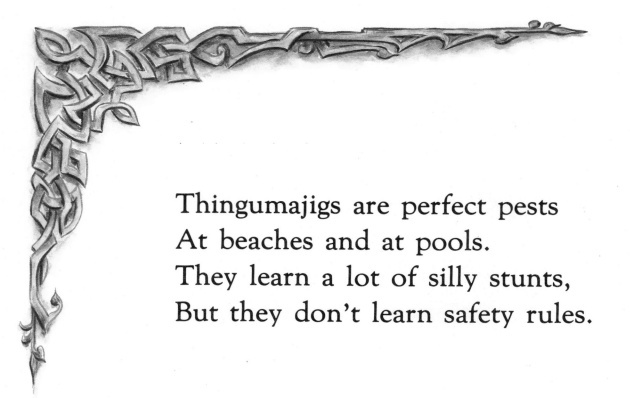

Thingumajigs are perfect pests
At beaches and at pools.
They learn a lot of silly stunts,
But they don't learn safety rules.

Swim near the lifeguard
Close to the shore.
After eating,
Wait an hour or more.

LIFE GUARD

NEVER SWIM ALONE!

SWIM IN SAFE PLACES

Thingumajigs are featherheads—
They never watch the light.
Thingumajigs look up and down,
But they don't look left and right.

Look both ways.
Do it right.
Cross at the corner.
Wait for the light.

Thingumajigs climb on tables.
Thingumajigs climb on chairs.
Thingumajigs leave roller skates
Halfway up the stairs.

I think of others
When I play—
I always put
My toys away.

TOY BOX

They punch their neighbors,
And they sass their teachers.
But they pet strange dogs,
And they hug weird creatures.

They may look cute,
And they may look cuddly—
But they could be mean,
And they could be ugly!

Stay away from strange dogs!

They grab all the swings,
And they push on the slide.
They run around the playground
With their shoes untied.

I watch my step and wait my turn.
Safety rules are rules to learn.

In cars and trains and buses,
They fidget and they clown.
Thingumajigs hang out windows.
Thingumajigs won't sit down.

SAFETY FIRST!

Buckle up your seat belt.
Hands off the door.
Don't distract the driver.
Keep both feet on the floor.

Thingumajigs are runarounds
Who wander on their own.
They never learn their address or
The number of their phone.

Ask a
policeman.
He's your
friend.

NEVER TAKE
CANDY FROM
STRANGERS

They're careless in the kitchen.
They won't wipe up their spills.
They're all bad news at barbecues
Running round the grill.

Never play with matches.
This means you!
Stay away from stoves and knives.
That's a good rule too.

Thingumajigs eat jars of junk—
They live on chocolate candy.
They buy it by the bucketful
And always keep it handy.

Have fun. Feel good.
Drink your milk.
Eat wholesome food.

Thingumajigs don't bundle up—
Even when it's snowing.
They never read the warning signs.
And they don't watch
    where they're going.

Take care.
Dress right too.
Safety First!
It's up to you.

Thingumajigs don't exercise—
They hate it like the dickens.
They lie around on couches,
And they never walk their chickens.

Games are good for me and you.
We build our bodies
And have fun too.

They gobble sweets
    and sticky treats.
They think that pop is grand.
But Thingumajigs
    don't brush their teeth
And never wash their hands.

Healthy people
stay that way
with good health habits
every day.

Thingumajigs fuss
And Thingumajigs fight,
And they never get to bed
Till the middle of the night.

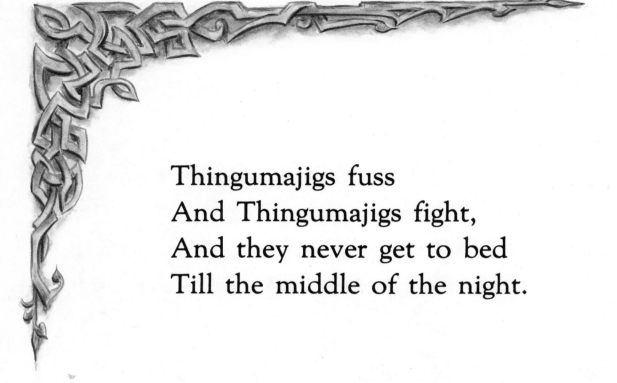

We need our rest

To do our best.

Go back to the beginning now
And take another look.
There's a whole lot to learn
In *The Thingumajig Book!*